The Buddha Taught Nonviolence, Not Pacifism

PAUL R. FLEISCHMAN, M.D.

Pariyatti Press ✳ Seattle

PARIYATTI PRESS
P.O. BOX 15926
SEATTLE, WASHINGTON 98115
WWW.PARIYATTI.COM

———————————✻———————————

ISBN: 1-928706-22-3

Printed In Canada

*For information about Vipassana meditation
as taught by S.N. Goenka,
including locations of Vipassana centers worldwide and
meditation course schedules, please see the website,*
www.Dhamma.org.

Contents

The Buddha Taught Nonviolence, Not Pacifism

In the wake of the terrorist attacks of September 11, 2001, I have found myself reflecting on nonviolence, its contributions, its limits, and its place in the Buddha's teaching. I have also been surprised to hear many of my acquaintances confuse the Buddha's teaching of nonviolence with pacifism. In their confusion about the difference, they find themselves either rejecting nonviolence as hopelessly naïve and inadvertently destructive, or embracing the politicized group allegiances of pacifism, which they imagine incorrectly to present what the Buddha taught.

The Buddha did not intend to form either a religious or political position, or a philosophy of society. Historically, he lived before the era of organized, systematic theorizing about the human collective. He addressed himself as an individual to individuals. Even when he spoke to large groups, as he frequently did, he focused on individual responsibility. He understood every group—for example, the democratic states that existed in the India of his times—as resting upon the insight, conscience, and actions of each of its participants. He had no theory of nor belief in supervening, collective structures of society or government that could amend or replace the bedrock of individual choice.

Rather than a theologian or a systems thinker, the Buddha was a liberator, a spiritually attained practitioner and teacher of the path to *nibbāna*—freedom from hate, delusion, and fear. His goal was to help as many beings as possible live in equanimity, harmony, and loving-kindness. He was against all belief systems—a position that confounded many of his contemporaries, and that still puzzles people today who want to understand what "ism," what philosophy, he propounded. Many people still yearn to find in his words some "Buddhist fundamentalism" by which they can anchor ideological convictions and security against the turmoil of life.

The "Dhamma," or path to liberation, for which the Buddha was spokesman, is not an idea; it is a mode of conduct and a way of life that leads to personal realization. Its goal is to release its practitioners from authorities and ideologies, not anarchistically or capriciously, but through training, by deepening their personal experiences of the nature of their true self and its ethical implications. It is through these long-cultivated, gradually deepening experiences that the Buddha led his followers to autonomy from ideas, philosophies, scriptures, even from himself. His classic similes focused on direct tangible experience. Like one from whom a poisoned arrow is removed, the student of Dhamma will experience relief from pain. Like one who eats nourishing food, the student of Dhamma will know the taste of liberation. These direct experiences of life's meanings and values are the Buddha's teaching. Just as the Buddha never did, many practitioners of Dhamma do not call themselves "Buddhists."

Yet morality is the first step on the path the Buddha taught. Why is morality given so much initial attention in a nonideological, experiential path?

In order to see oneself, to know oneself, to experience one's own true nature, one must focus observation repeatedly, continuously, as a lifelong practice, on who one really is. This lifestyle of awareness, meditation, and observation requires openmindedness—hence the Buddha's emphasis on freedom from rigid beliefs—but the path also requires patience, calmness, and integrity. To make mindful observations of oneself a way of life, one needs a steady, focused mind. This can only be obtained when honesty, harmony, modesty and sincerity are already adhered to. It is for this reason that whenever the Buddha taught Dhamma, he started with the five moral precepts: not to steal, lie, use intoxicants, commit sexual misconduct—and not to kill. Nonviolence is a prerequisite to, and the first step of the Buddha's teaching. It appears not as a belief, but as a practical necessity to the intentional and aware path of Dhamma. Initially, for the student of the Buddha, nonviolence is a psychological necessity for self-development.

However, this utilitarian and personal introduction to nonviolence as a moral precept is only the surface layer of the Buddha's teaching. Continuing to eschew ideology or philosophy, the Buddha's guidance was toward experiences that deepen discernment. Students are led to the point where they see themselves clearly through the practice of meditation. What happens then to the moral precept of nonviolence, when they have lived a way of life that directs them to encounter the transience of personal existence, the insubstantiality of ourselves, of our perceptions, of our viewpoints, of our history, of our world? Is there any value or meaning to nonviolence for small, temporary beings, born out of past causes, destined to live briefly then die, a passing aggregate of mind and matter scintillating for a moment in the vast corridors of endless time?

As a student of the Buddha matures on the path, he or she opens to new perspectives, and the mind becomes more able to see various viewpoints simultaneously. The path the Buddha taught is a deepening realization, without reduction to doctrine. Experiential apprehension of nonviolence replaces mere moral adherence to it. In the depth of realization of personal impermanence, certain truths become self-evident. All things are impermanent; all beings are transient; all beings suffer the common experiences of loss, decay, death. While each person, plant, or animal, has its own causes, its own seeds, that brought it into being, all share the bond of birth and death. Ultimately, nonviolence is a recognition of the simple facts that the quality of our life is the same as the quality of our moment-to-moment thoughts and feelings, and that enmity, hatred, and violence never improve our state of mind. Just as a man would not seethe with violence against his own body, he wouldn't harm himself by seething with violence . . . period. Liberation means non-violence. The Buddha's path begins with behavioral acquiescence to vows not to kill, but it culminates in an identification with nonviolence as the essence of what liberates the mind and heart from hate, fear, and self-promoting delusion. "All fear death. Comparing others with oneself, one should neither kill nor cause to kill." Nonviolence is the essence of what the Buddha taught. Nonviolence is liberating because, in each and every moment that it suffuses our minds—in those moments the mind feels compassion, identification, and empathy with other beings.

For the Buddha, nonviolence is a precept that enables the journey to express the root meaning of itself. Initially, the student obeys the precept of nonviolence. Eventually, he or she comes to embody nonviolence as a cherished tone quality of life.

II

Here are two key differences between nonviolence as taught by the Buddha, and pacifism. First, the Buddha did not teach social and political philosophy; and second, he taught a path of life, not a blanket ideology. Guiding each interested individual to walk the path, the Buddha encouraged a pure mind that seeks the least harm. He recognized different levels of personality development, different social roles and obligations, different responsibilities and necessities incumbent on different individuals according to their history and choices. The Buddha taught people according to their *kamma*. [Sanskrit: *karma*.]

As a member of the warrior caste, the Buddha maintained cordial relations with kings. Numerous *suttas* (discourses) in the Pāli Canon record his conversations with Kings

Pasenadi and Bimbisara. Shunning political involvement, the Buddha never advised his royal students to convert their kingdoms into democracies, despite the fact that many local states were in fact kingless republics. Although we have on record numerous discourses that the Buddha gave in the presence of, or even directly to, royalty, he never counsels them to abandon legal administration with its attendant consequences and punishments for crimes, nor to abandon warfare and protection of their state. In a poignant conversation that occurred when both the Buddha and King Pasenadi were eighty years old, the king praises the Buddha, his teaching, and the conduct of his followers, while describing himself as "an anointed warrior-king, able to have executed those who should be executed." The king comments with irony that despite his power people always interrupt him, while the Buddha's students listen attentively "without either punishment or weapon." And the king holds in awe the social order surrounding the Buddha, where meditators "enjoy concord . . . mingling like milk and water and regarding each other with kindly eyes. . . . I see nowhere else any assembly so harmonious."

After the king departs, the Buddha comments to the meditators around him that the king's insights were "monuments to the Dhamma" that should be learned and remembered as "fundamentals of the holy life." This passage clarifies that the Buddha neither condemned nor even rebuked the king for his fulfillment of the kingship, with all its dire responsibilities.

A similar window into the early and ancient interpretation of the Buddha's teaching comes from King Aśoka, who lived several hundred years after the Buddha. Aśoka is credited as being the greatest "Buddhist" king both in the extent of his influence and in the depth of his understanding of Dhamma, and he was responsible for the famous edicts carved in rock which constitute "the oldest surviving Indian written documents." These wise and humane passages, which imply a level of civilized conduct to which humankind still aspires, praise such virtues as self-examination, and religious tolerance. They are based on Dhamma—the universal path to liberation—and never mention Buddha or "Buddhism." Explicitly banning animal sacrifice (which had been the foremost religious ritual before the

Buddha's time), the edicts praise non-harmfulness but stop short of rigid absolutism: "Not to injure living beings is good." Aśoka's conversion to Dhamma led him to abandon military conquest (of which he had already done a lifetime's share), and to claim that "conquest by Dhamma is the only true conquest." But, according to an authoritative historian, he did not "abjure warfare, never abandoned armies... and he avoided disastrous pacifism, ... retaining the option of capital punishment." There is no reason to imagine that the Buddha ever encouraged those of his students who held administrative responsibilities to promulgate an anarchic abnegation of governmental function.

In a brief discourse, the Buddha is challenged by a general who claims that Dhamma is mere passivity. The Buddha replies that he teaches inactivity in regard to unwholesome things and "activity by way of good conduct in deeds, words, and thoughts." There is no further blanket position taken towards government, warfare or the *kamma* of generals. What constitutes good conduct is left to the general's discernment. The Buddha gave the principle, not the details of the infinite varieties of interpretation and application.

The interrelation between *kamma*, role choice, and warfare is illustrated in the history of India. An ancient Greek historian named Megasthenes arrived in India as an ambassador and traveled widely, recording his observations in approximately 300 BC—after the Buddha's death, but even before Aśoka's reign of Dhamma—while the Buddha's influence still remained strong in North Indian civilization. Megasthenes describes two armies fighting while farmers plowed nearby "in perfect security." How different this is from the wars of invasion into India by Mahmud of Ghazni around 1000 AD, in which the invader took pride in slaughtering 50,000 civilians in a day and burning their civilization to extinction. Mahmud's chronicles boasted of the extent of the destruction of temples, buildings and all infrastructure—an obliterative conquest. Several hundred years later, Muhammad of Ghor campaigned through northern India leaving "scenes of devastation and massacre... all that was sacred in religious or celebrated in art was destroyed"—a "culture-icide" that eliminated the last rays of the Buddha's teaching from northern India. This was similar to the fervor of extermination that accompanied the European domination over the Americas, or Nazi genocide. Clearly, warfare was not eliminated from the cradle of the Buddha's teaching but, under the penumbra of his presence, it developed a temporary delimitation and constraint foreign to most other civilizations.

Mr. S. N. Goenka, a contemporary teacher of Dhamma who attempts to keep the teaching pure, neither adding nor deleting anything from the Buddha's way, sees no conflict in teaching Dhamma to police or to military personnel. His purpose is not to induce them to quit their jobs, but to encourage government servants to more humanely fulfill their functions with firmness and without feelings of hate or revenge. The soldier who has also begun to embrace Dhamma aims to become an upholder of justice, not a hired killer.

Similarly, men who have risen to high governmental authority but who have tried to live the life of Dhamma, like U Nu of Burma, have spoken about the need to skillfully ascertain the difference between moral absolutes and the flexibility required by the multiple functions of modern governments.

This includes assessing when and where not-killing might actually be a form of implicit violence, echoing Gandhi's view.

None of this, however, justifies hatred, or violence in service of personal goals or gains. For the government servant who, for example, as a soldier, must kill, the Buddha implicitly asks of him two questions. The first is: "Can you do this task as an upholder of safety and justice, focused on love of those you protect rather than on hate for those you must kill?" If you are acting with vengeance or delight in destruction, then you are not at all a student of Dhamma. But if your hard job can be done with a base of pure mind, while you are clearly not living the life of an enlightened person, you are still able to begin walking the path towards harmony and compassion. The Buddha's ethics clearly allows differentiation between the actions of Allied soldiers fighting to liberate Auschwitz and other death factories at the end of World War II and the actions of mass murderers.

However, the Buddha's teaching implies a second question for soldiers, police and for all of us: "Are you prepared to proceed further on the path toward mental purity and enlightenment?"

III

Fundamental to the Buddha's teaching is the concept of volition or *kamma*. Our quality of life is a product of our choices. Every major choice in life entails commitments, limitations, and consequences. Although no consequence is permanent—because liberation from all *kamma* is possible, though it may take lifetimes, even millions of them!—a man who accepts the kingship or who becomes a soldier also accepts the responsibilities incumbent upon the role. He can be a good king and improve his own lot as he provides security and justice to his subjects, and he can meditate and thereby take steps on the Path of Dhamma, but he cannot claim the exemptions and privileges of a *bhikkhu*. Implicitly, the Buddha asks us all to examine our fundamental position in life, our deepest choices.

The term *"bhikkhu"* has often been translated to mean "monk," and there are numerous passages in the Pāli Canon where that is the probable meaning; but in the Dhammapada the Buddha defined *bhikkhu* as a committed student of Dhamma, with a lifelong practice of moral precepts, meditation, and the cultivation of purity. The Buddha clearly included serious and committed lay persons in his lectures to *bhikkhus.* In the Dhammapada, *bhikkhu* is defined as unrelated to the external forms of appearance or to membership in a particular religious order. Even a well dressed nobleman riding an elephant (the pre-eminent status symbol of wealth and authority) is a *bhikkhu* if he lives in peace, meditates, cultivates purity of mind and "lays aside the rod toward all living beings."

According to the Buddha, a committed student of his path, a *bhikkhu*, by definition, practices nonviolence, but those who have not chosen this role may or must, fulfill other social roles and follow other precepts. The Buddha's teaching asks us all to consider whether we are ripe to take up the responsibilities and limits incumbent on the life of a committed practitioner of Dhamma.

Therefore, while the Buddha never lectured at his longtime student King Pasenadi to forsake his throne, when the aging king felt death closing in on him he concluded, with the help of the Buddha's questioning, "There is no scope or use for battles when aging or death are closing in . . . what else can I do but walk in Dhamma?" So different choices are appropriate for different people and for different life stages of the same person. The Buddha respected and befriended King Pasenadi while he remained king, and the king mirrored that mutual respect and persevered as a student of the Buddha while continuing with royal prerogative and problems; until the king, based on his own insight and volition, ripened to a new level of commitment to Dhamma and to nonviolence.

It is to serious meditators who are committed practitioners of moral precepts, daily meditation, and a purified mind, that the Buddha gave his stunning, often quoted, guidance on nonviolence, "Even if bandits brutally severed him limb from limb with a two-handled saw, he who entertained hate in his heart on that account would not be one who followed my teaching." Please note that this famous passage does not preclude skillful and vigorous self-defense that is free of hate.

Bandits and terrorists act from deforming pain. This mind full of tormenting venom evokes our compassion, though not our permission. While aware of his disease, we may halt the bandit with force. A student who was absorbed in a ten-day meditation course overlapping September 11, 2001, reported, upon emerging days later from his retreat: "I don't know why, but the first thing that crossed my mind when I heard . . . was a pity for the people who did it."

Committed meditators are defined not only by their serious practices of meditation and nonviolence, but they also "speak wisely . . . and explain the meaning of Dhamma." This describes an expressive, explanatory, educative aspect, to "walk in the world and teach Dhamma."

The sincere meditator is not only non-violent, but is also a witness to the nonviolent potential in daily living. As we saw earlier how the Buddha advised the general, this expresses "activity by way of the good." By example and in speech, the committed meditator seeks the least harm for all beings in all situations. On the other hand, this lifelong practitioner of Dhamma does not promote himself as a political leader. His witness is personal, exemplary and public, but neither power-seeking nor self-promotional. Two key criteria the Buddha imposed on himself and his followers were: never to speak for the sake of worldly advantage, and never allude to yourself.

According to the positions one has under-taken, different relationships to nonviolence evolve. The determined meditator purifies her mind so that all violence becomes impossible, but she does not automatically condemn the government servant who diligently seeks to ascertain justice while defending society against violence, and who is thereby occasion-ally called to the use of force. When asked whether a judge should abjure capital punishment, Mr. Goenka replied that the judge should uphold his legitimate judicial functions, while at the same time working for the long-term elimination of capital punishment.

The Dhamma is not an ideology but is a set of tools for assessing one's own volitions, responsibilities, feelings and behaviors, in order to align them with nonviolence according to one's abilities and capacities. As a group, serious practitioners of Dhamma form a voluntary set of devoted, nonviolent witnesses who ballast the reactive society around them. The Buddha's teaching of nonviolence for serious meditators makes them, properly defined, what the American Selective Service calls "conscientious objectors" to war.

IV

Freud echoed conventional wisdom when he wrote that civilization consists of good conduct despite the wayward unconscious trends of the human mind. The Buddha stepped outside of convention when he insisted that the mind, not conduct, was the true target of transformation. For him, nonviolence is an essential rule, a culmination of a meditative way of life, a product of individual choice and position, and a nonstop, nonsituational way of being. Here is another key difference between the Buddha's nonviolent position and pacifism: nonviolence is continuous, a pervasive and quotidian effort. Before and after any war, before and after outbreaks of violence, the student of Dhamma, the committed meditator, lives the life of nonviolence toward his friends, acquaintances, animals, trees and food. He even "holds himself aloof from causing injury to seeds or plants."

The student of Dhamma seeks the least harm at all times. Realistically, as a surgeon she may have to incise her patient's body, or as a police officer arrest the armed robber, or as a teacher discipline the unruly student. Realistically, in the ambiguous rough-and-tumble of the householder's life and public discourse, the student of Dhamma may need to make difficult decisions, take unpopular stances, and even utter unflattering sentences. He or she will be called upon also to recognize the complexity and ambiguity that rests on the shoulders of those who have positioned themselves to make decisions in a world of turmoil and suffering. But the sincere devotee of Dhamma understands that the goal of every moment is to generate empathy and compassion, to minimize anger and hate. This double layer is part and parcel of the Buddha's teaching: to simultaneously generate skillful, maximally beneficial conduct in addition to affiliative, nonretaliatory feelings of identification toward the people one has to deal with. Nonviolence is only the surface layer of a heart of love and compassion. Few honest people can say they feel nothing else, but for the student of the Buddha's path, for the practitioner of Dhamma, a pure heart is the goal of every moment, no matter how many thousands of times one's real feelings fall short of this ideal.

Due to this focus on volition, Dhamma awakens its practitioners to continuously assess one's own state of mind, and not just to act. What appears to be noble restraint from retaliation may only be fear or expeditious tactics. What appears to be strong defense of helpless people may only be ego-boosting aggression. The Buddha's primary focus on intention allows him to consider a proper role for benign force, as Dr. Olendzski has shown in his analysis of the Buddha's discussion of how a parent must act if a small child were choking on a pebble. In this case, even drawing blood could be compassionate. Nonviolence has room for strong actions whose origins rest in concerned and caring motives.

Similarly, passive, acquiescent enabling of violence is not Dhamma. We have seen how the Buddha reassured the general that Dhamma is not inactivity. We have also seen how speaking up on behalf of Dhamma is part of the definition of a committed meditator. If one truly understands that positive qualities of heart and mind constitute the path to enlightenment, and that the highest welfare for all beings is a life of harmony and peace, then permitting someone else to perpetrate harm without consequences is not non-violence.

For the committed disciple of the Buddha's path, it is essential not only to refrain from killing, but also to refrain from encouraging others to kill. The Buddha addressed this problem regarding vegetarianism, where the advice to accept whatever food is given to you sometimes contradicted the admonition not to kill or cause animals to be killed. The conclusion to this problem was: one should never eat meat of an animal killed intentionally on one's behalf, since this would be encouraging others to kill; but if meat is already present in food not specifically prepared for you, but now offered to you, one should just accept the gift as given. This quaint example shows both the seriousness of the concern not to induce others to kill, but also the pragmatism and flexibility with which it was interpreted. How does this apply to followers of the Buddha, who encourage the police or army to protect the civil order? Aren't they encouraging others to kill on their behalf? Conversely, if the practitioner of Dhamma passively allows, permits or facilitates violence, isn't this encouraging the violent perpetrator on his destructive and downward course?

The Buddha's path of nonviolence guides us through a personal scrutiny, not a pat answer. Taking systematic meditation as our most penetrating tool we must decide how to avoid killing, and how to be spokespersons for Dhamma—neither violent nor passive. To the extent that one has extracted oneself from lifestyles of force—such as military service— and to the extent that Dhamma has become a committed way of life, then the Buddha's answer, by speech and example, is unambiguous. The Buddha promoted nonviolence by spreading Dhamma in its fullness, not by political activity or "single issue" thinking. Through exemplary lifestyle, through self-restraint, through verbal explanation, the follower of the Buddha acts on behalf of the good.

The historical record contained in the Pāli Canon describes the Buddha as finding a middle path between involvement in specific political issues—which he never did—and complicitous acceptance of injustice—which he also attempted to avoid. Never a direct critic of particular governments or policies, he was assertive and forthright in teaching Dhamma, the way of life.

As a concerned, involved, nonaligned citizen, the Buddha was proactively expressive. He focused on profound, complete confirmation of ultimate human potential, rather than on compromised expediency. He challenged unproved attestations and impractical speculations. In particular, he criticized "eternalism," which postulates an eternal essence or soul in an eternal universe. He specifically chided passive prayer. He never made calculated equivocations to woo a constituency. He did not compromise on what he knew, and on what—he dared to emphasize—no one knows (like who or what "created the universe"). He did not apologize for other people's ethnocentric or nationalistic belief systems in order to gain alliance with them. He punctured the fallacies of divine intervention, or hedonistic cynicism, in direct verbal challenge. The Buddha simultaneously emphasized that the Dhamma is not intended for "criticizing or refuting others in disputation," but neither is it an acquiescence to any dogma about the Self or the Universe.

He called his a "Teaching for the removal of all grounds for views of all prejudices, obsessions, dogmas and biases."

Ultimately, one who practices right speech is described by the Buddha: "Thus does he live as one who binds together those who are divided . . . a peacemaker, a lover of peace . . . a speaker of words that make for peace." Well spoken speech has five marks: it is timely, true, gentle, purposeful, and kindhearted. While the Buddha is described as participating in public presentations of his experiential, dogmaless Dhamma, and thereby disagreeing with other peoples' practices or traditions, he never did so with an oppositional, conversional fervor. He did not raise the excited prophetic banner of charismatic religion. He expressed his nonviolent ethic but he did not campaign for it. His tone, topic, and style were uniform.

On one occasion, a king sent his envoy to the Buddha for advice. The king's envoy was explicit: the king intended to "annihilate and utterly destroy" the free, democratic country of the Vajjis—what did the Buddha think? Instead of answering directly, the Buddha turned to his disciple Ānanda and interviewed him about the state of affairs among the Vajjis, establishing whether they continued to adhere to the teaching that the Buddha had previously given to them to insure their growth as a people. This teaching consisted of seven conditions, the essence of which is the creation of a conservative, reverential, coherent society that assembles peaceably and regularly and respects women and elders. Recognizing the vitality and strength of the Vajjis, the genocidal king's envoy returns to the capitol with the advice not to attack them. While there may be some idealistic hopes unfulfilled in this prophecy—for in short order all the democratic republics of India were destroyed by kingdoms—it reveals to us the Buddha's styles and beliefs. He refrained from political involvement and focused his attention on principles rather than specifics, placing social safety upon harmony, discourse, traditional rules, and civic involvement, and frequent and peaceable assemblies. The Buddha by analogy then applied these same seven guidelines to the community of *bhikkhus* (whose harmonious relations King Pasenadi had found so notable) for their longevity and prosperity—a positive outcome still bearing fruit after thousands of years.

V

The historical dispensation of the Buddha occurred in a pastoral country where news spread by word of mouth. His teaching emphasized perspective, realization of how we tend to overemphasize ourselves, our time, our place, and our personal sensations. The Dhamma he expounded is an attempt to be realistic, to see things in their true proportions and to activate nonviolence practically.

Today we live in the center of multiplying spheres of attention. The Buddha never addressed many of the social issues that are thrust upon our daily consideration. The attempt to find situational guidance from the Buddha for our personal conundrums misuses his teaching, creating "Buddhism"—an ideology—in the place of Dhamma—a lifelong, guided, personal experience. In facing the violence of September 11, 2001, practitioners of Dhamma cannot escape into books where the Buddha will tell them what to believe. In seeking to apply nonviolent attitudes, questions—not doctrines—will arise.

What are the dimensions and contexts of terrorism? How do they compare to other forces of destruction that do not have media attention? Do the thousands of deaths at the World Trade Center merit the same attention as the 30,000 people who die in the United States every year by suicide—personal terrorism that gets little attention? How do these deaths compare to the guesstimate of 300,000 deaths per year in the United States secondary to the preventable complications of obesity? What about the approximately 50,000 who die in violent auto accidents annually? Will violence against the environment eventually eliminate human life entirely?

What is religious freedom? In the United States religious freedom is limited: members of the Church of Jesus Christ of Latter-day Saints (Mormons) were not allowed to practice religiously sanctioned polygamy. What other religious beliefs and practices might be incompatible with the dignity of individuals or with the rights of other persons? Is "canonically obligatory holy war against other religions" a doctrine with which democracy can coexist? Is the relentless and enormous violence associated with organized religion intrinsic to it? Are we in denial regarding the dangers of blind faith the way that certain African and Asian countries deny the AIDS epidemic, due to which their citizens continue to die from a preventable illness? Was Gandhi's religious pacifism in 1947 one component among many that were responsible for the violence that accompanied the partition of India and Pakistan during which the most fatal spontaneous nonmilitary slaughter in world history occurred?

Are individual terrorist acts essentially different from collective terrorism, a culture of terrorism? After the Columbine High School murders in Colorado, tens of thousands did not dance for joy in Islamabad, Jakarta, and Gaza—does that change the fundamental nature of nonviolent response to political versus a personal terrorist massacre?

"If they are so angry at us, there must be a reason." Is the rape victim therefore to blame for the rape? This blaming-the-victim logic— does it apply to the Serbian rape camps in the Bosnian war, or to the "comfort girls" enslaved by the Japanese military in World War II? Was the military force that was eventually brought to bear against these mass sexual tortures itself violence, or humane rectification of violence? If American foreign policy is blamed for the September 11 attacks, is that also blaming the victim? Did the Native Americans get what they deserved based upon their foreign policy towards the European invaders of the Americas?

Where does responsibility intersect with complicity? If nonviolent witnesses object to military response to mass terrorism because it will lead to more deaths, do they also object to the police department remaining in existence, since the attempt to capture criminals also may lead to more deaths? Conversely, if military response is sometimes deemed acceptable, where or when will the cycle of self-justifying violence escalate beyond control of any kind? By what universal and non-self-deluding criteria can violence ever be called "acceptable?"

Is "bystander error" violence or non-violence? When surrounding nations allowed Hitler to liquidate Jews and Stalin to eliminate entire ethnic communities, was the initial restraint from war an act of peace or violence? When the United States used the examples of

World War II to launch bombing campaigns in Bosnia and then in Kosovo, was that compassionate police action or escalation of violence? Should the Northern States have severed relations with the slave-holding South in nineteenth century America, thus avoiding the staggering half-million deaths of the Civil War but at the cost of perpetuating slavery? If some airline hostages attack their hijackers, causing their own deaths and those of all others on the airplane in the ensuing crash, should we condemn the violence of their action or admire their bravery in averting what would have been much greater carnage in the end?

We cannot look to the Buddha to answer these questions. But his committed followers, relentless proponents of nonviolence, are beholden to avoid mass propaganda, politically correct intimidation, and sentimental simplifications. Nonviolence is not blind faith in fantasy solutions, but considered, thoughtful, effortful, sincere concern to pluck nonviolent contributions out from among the surging complexities of human social existence.

VI

We now see the Buddha's teaching of nonviolence as a sieve, through which his students filter the particles of reality. To the extent that one is committed to the path, everything must be passed through this sieve, which demands of us the examination of our choices, our motives, our chosen roles, our actions, and our inactions. In response to one event—for example, the terrorist attacks of September 11, 2001—different sincere followers of the Buddha's way may find themselves arriving at different positions, because each of them is working with a mirror of self-insight rather than with a political formulation. One Dhamma practitioner may see force as the best method of saving the most lives; another may see force as misguided revenge. In fact, in the complex series of actions that followed, force may have indeed operated both as preservation against further destruction as well as a vengeful retaliation. For all practitioners of Dhamma however, the core questions are the same: "How can I, given my position, abilities, development, and flaws, best bring to bear nonviolence in my wishes, word, and deeds?" The ethics of a committed meditator spring from a whole life of the practice of self-examination. Lacking one fixed relationship to state or government, the lifelong Dhamma practitioner may move between cooperation, distance, witness and correction.

Even with the vivid example of the Buddha's life and his clear verbal discourses, the Dhamma is not easy to apprehend because it does not conform to thought systems or preconceptions. Though it emphasizes right action in society, it differs from issue-specific politics or social work. Though it emphasizes nonviolence, it differs from pacifism. It is a systematic teaching that places nonviolence at the cornerstone of its foundation, but it is unaligned with government, movements or religions. It is knowable only as a way of life embedded in meditative insight. It is often described as an absence rather than a presence—an absence of hate, ill will and delusion, an absence of viewpoints and beliefs. It is a clearing away of the self-absorption which is the root of suffering.

The Buddha never claimed he could bring peace to the whole world. The narcissistic time scales of the prescientific scriptures of the West never occurred to him. He saw that suffering beings are limitless in time and space. The Buddha speaks to us from his position within an endless universe in which our current struggles for peace are not triumphal but eternal. But he also rejects defeatism or cynicism and promises this: a practical path to reduce suffering, which includes a generous dispensation of itself to others.

Nonviolence as the Buddha taught it was directed at each interaction in each moment but was not a comforting myth for denying inescapable truths. Dhamma is a long path, a footpath, culminated by only the rare few, and not a fantasy exit from the exigencies of the human condition. There are no global solutions even hinted at anywhere in the Buddha's dispensation of Dhamma. His followers practice nonviolence because it anchors them in alertness and compassion, expresses and reinforces their own mental purification, builds identification with other beings— human, animal, even seeds; and because it is their most cherished realization: mind matters most. Cultivation of love, peace and harmony is always the only irrefutable doctrineless meaning that people can experience.

The Buddha's teaching survives in the experience of those who practice the path he described and not in the verbal preservation of his words. In his often quoted talk to the independent peoples of Kālāma, he sounds what today we call the modern temper by emphasizing the ultimate authority of personal realization, above that of texts. In fact the ancient texts from twenty-five centuries ago are framed in echoingly distant contexts. Nevertheless, eternal truths sparkle within the old bedrock. They nowhere contain the self-inflated magical thinking that mistakes an earnest wish for world peace as if it were the actual harbinger of it. Instead they stress a disciplined lifestyle and contagion by example. Even though the Buddha exhorts us to live the message and not just read the words, the Pāli Canon contains bas reliefs of an enduring kingdom of peace that has already existed and can be called up from the heart of anyone who walks the path. As Pablo Neruda wrote:

"the ancient kingdom survives us all"

In times of war and times of peace—every day—the committed meditator dwells in love and compassion, radiated outward to all. To those who are alive, or who once were, or who will be; to those who are human or to other living beings; to those who intend good and to those who intend harm, not agreement but loving-kindness is sent.

It is through devotion to nonviolence as a compass that one sees a glimmering of *nibbāna* along the horizon. Who would prefer a heart of hate to a heart of peace?

Peace Is a State of Mind

For a Twenty-first Birthday in Times of War

I

There is a peace that hovers
              beyond the confines of words
              and language,

But which speaks when any person
              guides his gestures
              with the same solicitude
              as he would his infant son.

There is a peace mingled in the emptiness
              that enfolds all matter.

It becomes embodied in any person
              who observes her own mind
              as if it were her infant daughter
              toddling towards the open door.

People cannot bring peace to the earth.
              People cannot forge it like a
              blade nor crack its core and
              release its radioactive blaze.

Peace will arrive when sermons stop,
                when missionaries of every creed
                and of every degree
                get converted to the simple truths
                that defy all books and buildings.

Peace will bowl us over like summer surf
                when we stop holding on
                to religion, nationality, ethnicity,
                or gender.

Peace is felt as the universal gift of life and death
                that unites all living beings.

Peace runs free outside the corrals
                of compartmentalized identity.

Peace will shower down upon us
                like a corona of autumn leaves
                in our ripening years;

In those golden days every person will meditate
                in quiet self-contentment
                dawn and dusk
                like gleaming orbs reflecting
                the arising and declining sun.

The only scripture left will be one line:

    "Discern what helps; refrain from harm;
            purify your mind."

II

The old generations of peace pick their way
                along the middle path
                between the dichotomies.

They have no uniforms or creeds; they do not
                grab lecterns and limelights.

They wend long trails past timidity,
                avoiding those who rationalize
                compliance as peacemaking
                or acquiescence
                as dialogue and compromise.

When the windstorm strikes,
                every leaf flickers downward
                on its own fated, final course.

Coyotes howl in the night in troops;
                the owls, alone.

In the noisy hours of catastrophe
                the airwaves and street corners fill
                with self-proclaimed priests and
                prognosticators;

But there are ancient footprints
            leading on a path of peace
            where the staunch
            and uninfluenceable grey ones
            lean on their staffs for a breather
            and then walk on
            following the unmistakable
            single file track.

III

In the quiet days, the villagers believe
        the unruffled flow
        signifies deep clean water.

Those who watch the river carefully
        know the forces of destruction
        have never left this earth.

Minds with scars continue to plot their holy wars
        in the still-swirling
         eddies and currents,
        and the water is always red
        with silt and clay.

You cannot sift the river with ideas.
        You cannot puncture it
        to cleanse it.

The deep upwelling springs of peace
        are never situational or acute;
        they never bring the water to a boil.

They join the great river unnoticed,
               cooling drops from
               an undistinguished hill,
They travel in accreting clines
               of unhurried purity,
Confident that the water
               in its basic element is pure.

IV

The Buddha gave only one prescription,
                not war, not pacifism either.

Did you imagine the Buddha as a yielder,
                as a syncophant,
                as someone toadying
                to the unrepentant murderer
                and so endorsing some murder more?

Did you imagine the Buddha strategic,
                building alliance with tyrants
                to keep the current calm,
                claiming unprincipled enabling
                as peacemaking?

The Buddha spoke his mind, made his point,
                never coddled, never aligned,
                never equivocated to sound
                acceptable or in fashion.

He upbraided every view.

The peace he taught was to actively dispel
              delusion from oneself and from
              those who could follow well.

He advised nonviolence for those who plunged
              into a lifelong effort,
              a whole embracing way.

He taught a lifetime path
              to shape a new humanity
              starting with oneself
              and spread by inspirational
              example.

He did not prescribe that humankind lie down
              before the demonic,
              the jihads and the crusades.

He did not say that peace would ooze out
              of the apologists who quickly fawn
              to butchers in the act of butchery.

He vigorously rebuked eternalists who claimed
              their opinions sprang
              from imaginary gods.

In all his discourses to kings and nobles
              he never disparaged
              good judges and good generals.

Peace is not a homily that the comfortable and
               secure dictate from on high
               down onto the heads
               of anguished victims.

Peace will not be lassoed to our shins this year,
               this decade, this era.

Peace is a long, long path; our bodies are its
               stepping stones;
               our minds are its herbiage
               grown from long composted soil.

There are fungi that glow in the forest in the
               night;

There are birds that cross all meridians
               by moonlight;

There are ochre beams that bathe the burning
               earth in their softening touch;

There are people meditating tonight who rebuff
               the barrage of black books
               that are rocking the ark of the world.

V

I put my faith in you, young mothers who are
                nursing babies.

I put my faith in you, empiricists
                whose sense of time
                transforms the galaxies into
                fireflies.

I put my faith in all of you who are scientific
                and rational,
                who speak up clearly about
                the limits of conviction
                and the known.

It is through self-importance that people
                delude themselves into beliefs.

Wherever humans howl, a self-appointed,
                self-important idea
                empowers their entitlement.

Hate is the appendix of earnest ideology.

Peace is a state of mind that antedates ideas
of any kind.

The mind can never find peace, but peace returns
to the letting-go mind
as a child runs to greet
his returning mother.

VI

Meditate on the transience of sensations
　　　　　of the self.

Let go of yourself one hundred thousand times.

Autumnal sugar maples turn audacious scarlet,
　　　　　russet, and carmine hues,

But roots are the trees' true nurture,
　　　　　serene in seasonless sure soil
　　　　　beneath the coral cycles of the
　　　　　leaves.

Meditate with friends, or alone, or with the dead,
　　　　　or with the unborn.

Pour the honeyed tea of your long-steeped
　　　　　perspective into cups
　　　　　of as many guests as visit
　　　　　your out-of-the-way kitchen.

Peace flows from person to person when
　　　　　whole lives doff delusion
　　　　　to watch bare reality unfold.

Meditate in a peace that transcends
　　　　　even your own misunderstanding.

References

Page

10   *All fear death* . . . Dhammapada, 129

14   . . . *an anointed warrior-king . . . fundamentals of the holy life."* Majjhima-nikāya, 89

15   . . . *the oldest surviving Indian written documents* . . . Basham, A.L., *The Wonder That Was India*, 1954, p. 53

16   *Not to injure. . .only true conquest* . . . Rhys Davids, T.W., *Buddhist India*, 1903, pp. 294-297

16   . . . *abjure warfare* . . . Keay, J., *India: A History*, 2000, p. 92

16   . . . *activity by way of good conduct* . . . Aṅguttara-nikāya, Book of Eights, 46

17   . . . *in perfect security* . . . Keay, p. 94

17   . . . *scenes of devastation* . . . Keay, pp. 209, 213, 238

18   . . . *men who have risen* . . . King, W.L., *In the Hope of Nibbāna*, 1964, pp. 277-279

22   . . . *the Buddha defined* bhikkhu . . . Dhammapada, 142 & 362; see also Dīgha-nikāya, 13

23 *There is no scope or use for battles* . . . Majjhima-nikāya, 21

23 *Even if bandits* . . . Majjhima-nikāya, 26

24 *. . . speaks wisely* . . . Dhammapada, 363

25 *Two key criteria* . . . Aṅguttara-nikāya, Book of Fives, 12

28 *. . . holds himself aloof* . . . Dīgha-nikāya, 13

29 *. . . how a parent must act* . . . Olendzki, A., "Healing or Harming" in *Insight,* Fall/Winter, 2001. This contains a discussion based on the Abhayarāja Kumāra Sutta, Majjhima-nikāya, 58

32 *. . . chided passive prayer* . . . Dīgha-nikāya, 13

32 *. . . criticizing or refuting* . . . Majjhima-nikāya, 22

33 *Teaching for the removal* . . . ibid.

33 *Thus does he live* . . . Dīgha-nikāya, 13

33 *Well spoken speech has five marks* . . . Aṅguttara-nikāya, Book of Fives, 17

33 *On one occasion* . . . Dīgha-nikāya, 16

34 *. . . democratic republics . . .destroyed* . . . Rhys Davids, pp. 40-41

44 *. . . talk to the . . . Kālāmas* . . . Aṅguttara-nikāya, Book of Threes, 65

45 *. . . the ancient kingdom* . . . Neruda, Pablo, *Selected Poems,* trans. Tarn, et al., Boston, 1970, p. 187

48 *Discern what helps* . . . Dhammapada, 183

Karma and Chaos

Karma and Chaos explores the interface between psychiatry, science and the timeless teaching of the Buddha. Eight new and collected essays in this thoughtful work probe the heart of the Buddha's legacy to humanity: self-correction through meditation.

Drawing on his many years of practice as a therapist, and as meditation student and teacher, he guides us with authority and humility into the essence of Vipassana meditation as taught by S.N. Goenka, its psychological benefits and perils, and the inextricable foundation of moral actions.

ISBN 0-9649484-5-1
softcover, 150 pages; $12.95

Cultivating Inner Peace

The author holds up examples of people who have inspired him in his personal quest for harmony and happiness. Life sketches of such diverse exemplars as Helen and Scott Nearing, the Shakers, Walt Whitman, Gandhi, John Muir, Thoreau and Rabindranath Tagore demonstrate that it is a dispassionate equipoise in the face of everyday suffering that leads to inner peace. His ultimate example is an autobiographical account of his own experience with his practice of Vipassana. The final chapter of the book is a compelling appeal to all people to walk the path of peace as a way of healing the earth itself.

ISBN 0-87477-860-3
hardcover, 300 pages; $16.00